Five-a-Side Football

Five-a-Side Football

A guide to mini football

by Glenn Hoddle

with the assistance of Keir Radnedge

Pelham Books · London

First published in Great Britain by
Pelham Books Ltd
44 Bedford Square
London WC1B 3DP
1984

Hoddle, Glenn
  Five-a-side football
  1. Five-a-side soccer
  I. Title   II. Radnedge, Keith
  796.334'8   GV943.9.F5

ISBN 0 7207 1510 5

ERRATUM

The pictures on page 22 have been transposed:
traditional studs are shown in the picture
on the left.

Typeset by Cambrian Typesetters, Aldershot, Hants.
Printed in Great Britain by
Hollen Street Press Limited, Slough
and bound by Hunter & Foulis Limited, Edinburgh.

Contents

Acknowledgements

I would like to thank Tottenham Hotspur FC for the use of the facilities at White Hart Lane and my brother Carl Hoddle for his help with the photographs.

Picture Credits

The photographs in this book are reproduced by kind permission of All-Sport Photographic pages 10–11, 17, 19, 22, 23, 25, 28, 29, 31, 34, 35, 37, 41, 42, 45, 47, 48, 50,52, 53, 57, 59, 65, 69, 75; BBC Hulton Picture Library page 70; Press Association page 71; Sportapics Ltd page 74; Bob Thomas pages 14–15, 38, 39, 43, 73.

1

The Case for Five-a-Side

There is no greater game in the world than Association Football. From the beaches of Copacabana in Brazil to the steppes of Central Asia you will find children — and plenty of older 'children' — kicking a ball around.

The world federation, FIFA, boasts nearly forty million players registered with clubs and federations around the world. That's roughly one person in every hundred on this earth.

But for every 'registered' player, there are dozens to whom a football match is part of their recreation and entertainment and who don't figure in the official statistics. Their football is not necessarily the organised variety. It's spontaneous, born of a few minutes to spare and a yard or a patch of waste ground. The number of players doesn't matter, either. You don't need an exact eleven-a-side to enjoy football. The mere challenge of one man or boy against another with the ball between them is enough. It doesn't matter whether the man in possession, or the one making the tackle, has ten team-mates or two.

The sensation is enough; the sensation which is shared by kids in a playground, by workers in their lunch break and by the professional superstars in the World Cup Final — from the game's back waters to its very pinnacle.

To share a love of football is also to share an ambition: the will to improve, to progress, to increase one's level of skill and understanding. Whether your name is Joe Smith, Glenn Hoddle or Diego Maradona that's something which unites everyone who plays the game. And that's why I am writing this book. Because, while organised eleven-a-side soccer is the stuff of convention, it isn't the only expression of the game.

Five-a-side football has long been drawing crowds annually

to Wembley Arena for tournaments between some of England's most famous clubs and players; it is also the means by which the Americans – in an expanded version with six-a-side – are slowly learning the beauties of the game. But whether five-a-side or six-a-side there is more to this scaled-down version of soccer than public entertainment. In these mini forms every player can learn more, and prepare with special concentration for the conventional form of association football.

So there are the two elements of 'mini' football: the five or

A capacity crowd at Wembley Arena for the *Standard*'s 1984 five-a-side tournament.

six-a-side indoor and outdoor varieties as a form of spectacle; and the use of these formats as a training tool.

From my own experience I know the value of five-a-side. That was a lesson I quickly learned when I began going to Tottenham to train as an eleven-year-old. In fact the first time I took part in a televised football event was at the *Daily Express* National Five-a-Side Championships when I was sixteen. We were beaten in the final by Wolves, but I can still remember the thrill of appearing at Wembley – even if this was the covered arena, rather than the famous twin-

Growing up with Tottenham – I'm third from the right in the back row with the youth team.

towered stadium just across the huge car park. I had to wait a little longer to make that trip!

Some footballers can adapt to the demands of five-a-side better than others. I have always worked hard to improve my technique and I think that is one of the reasons why I have always enjoyed the close-pressure demands of the 'mini' game.

Technique and mobility are among the key qualities to successful indoor play and illustrate why I always remember Stan Bowles enjoying himself so much in these Wembley competitions. Stan won only five caps for England, but he had a high degree of skill which was of immense benefit indoors. He also, of course, had an impish element about his play which communicated itself to the crowds – particularly in an enclosed hall where the fans are so much closer to the players.

I think one of the problems in modern-day soccer is that much of the close relationship which once existed between players and fans has vanished. Nowadays plenty of parents prefer — because of fears of crowd trouble — to pay extra to take their sons to sit with them up in the stands, far away from the game. The players become anonymous, far-away figures and the personal link with the fans is further stretched towards breaking point. There are other reasons for falling attendances, of course, but it's no accident that five-a-side tournaments have remained immensely popular. And I don't believe that's just because of the pace and instant decision of such events. Certainly all the players I've come across throughout my career with Tottenham and England have enjoyed five-a-side work and the overall game can benefit.

When the Football League inaugurated their Soccer Six tournament at the National Exhibition Centre near Birmingham in the middle of the 1982-3 season they opened up vast possibilities for the British game. For years fans, players and officials have argued over ways and means to 'improve' the laws of the game to further the entertainment value and legislate against negative, defensive tactics. Now we saw a vehicle in which experiments could be made without jeopardising any of the established tournaments.

Whatever your feelings about a restriction of back-passing, use of a sin bin, abolishing throw-ins even, it must be admitted that the introduction of such innovations provided plenty of food for thought. Realistic thought, because now fans and officials had seen such ideas in use, and the players had tried them out.

I believe that the laws of the game have stood the test of time precisely because of the sound thinking which went into creating them and because they provide for an ideal balance between defence and attack. But that isn't to say that adjustments or minor improvements should not be made. I wouldn't like to see the law-making International Board suddenly throw over more than a century's work in favour of a series of major changes. But those elements which work successfully in indoor tournaments are clearly worth considering.

14

Action from the Football League's first Soccer Six tournament at the National Exhibition Centre, Birmingham, in January 1983.

For several years the West German federation experimented with time penalties and a sin bin in senior amateur football and were due to introduce this ice hockey-associated device into the *Bundesliga* in 1983-84. At the last moment, however, they got cold feet. But it may not be long before another country — for better or worse — does launch an extended top-level trial of the sin bin.

Football has maintained its popularity over the years as a game for spectators and players to enjoy because of its basic simplicity. It's all about getting the ball in the net.

In a restricted area that means plenty of movement and plenty of goals — and that adds up to entertainment. And it's the simplicity which means the game converts so well to five or six-a-side.

Surely British football will see more tournaments such as the Soccer Six event. An entire tournament can be completed in an evening. A lack of suitable indoor facilities might prove a problem. But I'm sure the fans would respond to a tournament pyramid which began with regional events in, say, Liverpool, Glasgow, Newcastle, Birmingham, London and Southampton, and which then moved to a national conclusion at Wembley Arena.

There is scope for expansion in competitive indoor mini football — and that can only be for the overall good of our game because the five-a-side variety is so valuable in training, practising and perfecting techniques for the eleven-a-side game. That doesn't just apply to outfield players, either. Goalkeepers benefit at least as much from five of six-a-side play. Fewer players means fewer defenders and therefore the goalkeeper comes under direct pressure much more often. In a League game he may have a shot to save once every five minutes — or even longer — on average. In a five-a-side match he'll probably be in action almost once a minute because of the speed with which play switches from end to end.

Five-a-side football can also help to mould your attitudes to match pressure and the big occasion. In a five-a-side game across half the training pitch — whether you're using full-size goals or the five-a-side 'scale models' — the chains of pressure are relaxed. That applies to full-time professionals as much as it does to part-timers, senior amateurs (though 'amateurs' don't officially exist any more!) and to boys whose

Sharpening up five-a-side techniques in the gymnasium at Tottenham.

Wembley or Hampden Park is in playing for their school.

Every player has his own skill level, but because he wants to improve he will try developing his technique in a five-a-side in a way he would not dare in a proper match. That applies to me as much as anyone.

Maybe I have been wrong over the years. Maybe I should have tried more spectacular work in matches. I have often wished that I could take into a League game the attitude with which I enter a five-a-side at Cheshunt – just that little bit more relaxed. Of course I want to win, whether I'm playing five-a-side on the training pitch or in the gymnasium or for England in the World Cup finals. But the difference is that if you lose at five-a-side you can go back into the changing rooms and it doesn't matter . . .

Pressure, in these terms, isn't the phone going all day with reporters chasing you or, for a manager, being top of the League. It's not even the fact that people pay money to see the team in action. Pressure is people actually being there watching you – in a big League or Cup game particularly. You have to go out with the right attitude, nerved to withstand the occasion, but relaxed enough to play your own game as best you can. And five-a-side can have much to do with getting that balance right.

If a trick or a nutmeg doesn't work in practice, that's all right, you can tell yourself, because this is only training work. But conversely, if a new addition to your skill repertoire works in the five-a-side then the feeling is fantastic – and that works wonders for your confidence. Confidence is half the sport. A confident player is a winning player. And again you can go back to the five-a-side basis to learn all about developing confidence.

Five-a-side is also a great help after injury. I learnt that lesson in the 1982-83 season. I had long spells out with ligament trouble both in an ankle and in a knee. The knee injury put me out for nine weeks and when I went back into training I started very gently, playing five-a-sides with the youth team. It was a frightening experience. I could still feel some pain in my knee and I thought: I'll never play again, because at first I was struggling to keep up with the youth team five-a-sides. I was scared to use my leg because of the injury and I just didn't feel on the same wavelength in terms of capability.

Slowly, painfully, the sharpness begins to come back. But a player just back from serious injury isn't up to real match practice. So it's in the five-a-sides that he gets back on the road to recovery. First with the youth team, then with the reserves, then with the first team. At each stage you feel you're struggling. But don't be despondent, don't give up. The injury is physical and heals. The problem is extending that healing process to influence your mental attitude. And, once more, those five-a-sides are invaluable.

Tottenham play more five-a-side-style football than most clubs, I think. During a busy season, when we go in for training during the week we will often play, say, eight-a-side for an hour, then do some running, and finish for the day. The hard stamina work has been done before the start of the season, so once we are under way it is a matter of keeping loose. That's the British way — but not every other country has yet discovered the magic of five-a-side.

In their early days at Spurs, Osvaldo Ardiles and Ricardo Villa were constantly commenting on this. Back in Argentina it appears that five-a-sides didn't take up much of training time. Work was built around running. They found our approach refreshing and stimulating because we were always able to get out on the pitch with a football.

And why not? That's all any footballer longs to do. . . .

2

Footwear and Other Equipment

Professional footballers are lucky where kit is concerned. Everything is provided by the club and leading players are generally fortunate enough to have boots supplied free by sponsoring manufacturers. But every player at first division level had to begin somewhere, had to buy his own boots, look after them and keep them in shape.

There is nothing more important than the right pair of boots. If you aren't comfortable, if you can't stand up properly or run securely then you can't express your own ability and you can't contribute one hundred per cent to the team effort.

Beware of false economy. That applies whether we are talking about the five-a-side game indoors or outdoors, six-a-side tournaments or eleven-a-side. The boots must be right!

Most First Division professionals have two sets of training boots and two sets of match boots. Why two sets? One set with normal studs for wet conditions and one set with rubbers to cushion the foot yet still provide a grip on a firm surface. They don't last long either. I reckon on getting through one pair of boots every six games. Maybe that gives you an idea of the pounding the boots take and consequently the importance of making sure you have the right pair. I remember one pair of boots lasted only three matches before I looked down during a game and saw a hole in the toe!

One rule about boots: never wear a new pair straight into a match. Wear them in during training first, preferably when it's wet so that the boot moulds more quickly and easily to your foot. Once I did wear a new pair of boots into a match, but I had so many problems and so much pain I would never do so again. So train in them first. A day when it's been raining really hard is just the time to get out there with those new boots!

 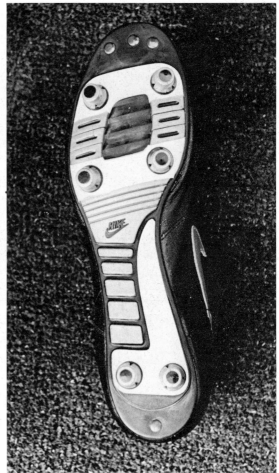

Left: Rubber soled training shoes and *Right*: traditional studs.

Opposite: Luton goalkeeper Andy Beasley, well protected in the London five-a-side at Wembley Arena.

But of course there is more to kit than boots, though they are of paramount importance.

Outfield players have no problems about general kit. But goalkeepers in five-a-side matches need to be prepared. For indoor play a goalkeeper needs to wear tracksuit trousers for protection – and that's not all. Elbow pads, knee pads and sometimes even thigh pads can be used to protect these vulnerable areas. Then, and only then, can a goalkeeper dive around his goal area with the sort of confidence you would expect from your regular professional on a wet Wednesday at Stoke.

Confidence is important for any player but particularly for goalkeepers whose role and responsibility is such that one misjudgment can break a team. If a goalkeeper hesitates for a split-second before moving, wondering whether he will hurt himself on landing, then it could already be too late and the ball could be in the net. Proper protection isn't only sensible self-interest — it's an important contribution towards the team effort.

As far as boots go, then the goalkeeper should wear the same as his team-mates. If it's wet outdoors, then studs; if it's firm, then rubbers. But indoor footwear is a different matter. It all depends on the surface — whether wood or concrete, or whether it's a form of artificial turf or 'carpet'. For wood or concrete ordinary training shoes are ideal, with a flat sole which provides a minimum amount of grip.

Artificial turf, however, demands special training shoes with soles which look almost like a magnified table tennis bat — plenty of pimples to sink into the carpet-like surface. You can use ordinary trainers on artificial turf — the so-called 'plastic grass' — and I can vouch for that from experience in the Arsenal gymnasium while working with the England squad. But the danger is that if your toe digs in, then you find your feet stopping sharply and you can topple forward. That in turn carries a risk of strains and pulls at the back of the leg and knee.

If you haven't got the right footwear it's like playing on ice. Correct footwear is essential. That was brought home to many players, officials and fans in the autumn of 1979 when England played a Wembley friendly against Czechoslovakia.

The Czechs, who often play in freezing and sub-zero temperatures during their own winter, took the precaution of bringing special footwear. That paid off because a cold snap meant large expanses of the Wembley turf were frozen and the Czechs commanded most of the first half. The England players changed into a variety of rubber soled boots and training boots at half-time and ended the game as 1—0 winners. But that victory was owed in large measure to the brilliance of Peter Shilton in goal and rammed home the lesson of the importance of correct footwear — and the need to be prepared.

Having the right boots isn't only a matter of being able to play to the best of your ability either. Your feet have to last

a long time — long after you've stopped playing football. So you must do all you can to protect them.

It might surprise the fan to know that professional footballers all suffer from blisters in pre-season training, even though we are all well aware of the importance of taking care of our feet. The constant pounding on hard ground during the summer can play havoc not only with your feet but with training schedules. Use bandages, plasters, Vaseline, soft soap — all that you can lay your hands on to try to protect the ankle, the back of the heel, the ball of the foot and your toes.

I often see kids playing in the parks in summer with ordinary boots on. I'm sure that's because they or their parents can't afford anything else. But if you *can* afford it, make sure you get the footwear right. It can make all the difference to your game — and remove much of the pain and the strain.

Bringing the Rules to Life

Formal or informal, outdoors or indoors, five-a-side football is different. To make the game both entertaining and instructive – whether a tournament or a training exercise – means adapting and adjusting the laws of the eleven-a-side game. The rules as laid down by the Football Association and by the Football League for their five and six-a-side tournaments are reproduced on pages 77-90.

Before going into a technical and tactical appreciation of the precise skills and schemes needed to benefit fully from the mini game, it's as well to be aware of the opportunities – and drawbacks — involved in cutting the game down to size.

The pitch

For organised five-a-side competition the pitch is roughly a third of the size of the normal outdoor field of play. The goals are half the width of the eleven-a-side variety and just over two-thirds of the height.

But the major difference in make-up is for indoor tournaments where the traditional touchline disappears. Instead, the wall surrounding the pitch is a part of it and so the ball is still in play when it rebounds or ricochets off this perimeter fence. The effect can be reproduced, of course, in a gymnasium for practice by school or fortunate youth-club players, and can prove valuable in developing control because of the odd angles at which the ball can suddenly arrive at a player's feet.

That's why players and coaches thinking in terms of mini football purely as a training tool would be unwise to ignore the 'wall game' if the facilities are available. Good technique is vital to good football and any methods which can help players improve their control should be pounced on! For training purposes, play *across* half a conventional pitch.

Above: To give you an idea of the size
of the five-a-side goal.

How to beat your man with the help
of the gymnasium wall.

Goal area

Although the dimensions differ, the rules for both five and six-a-side football provide a goalkeeper's area into which other players must not stray, on pain of a free kick.

This is a provision which can be sensibly used in five-a-side training sessions, though I have mixed feelings about the idea of a goalkeeper being handed permanent protection from the world about him.

Of course it suits the goalkeeper to know that no attacking player can get close enough in to take the ball round him. It also helps him because by noting the stride and progress of the attacking player, the goalkeeper is better able to judge the direction and timing of an eventual shot.

The goal area also helps the goalkeeper to concentrate on shot-saving knowing that he has little fear of coming under pressure while collecting crosses. For one thing the head-height rule means the ball must be kept down, for another no attacking players can rush him as he waits to collect a driven centre.

But while this has its value as a training exercise, I don't favour persistent use of a goal area for players whose minds are tuned to the eleven-a-side game. An attacking player needs experience of a one-to-one confrontation with a goalkeeper, just as a goalkeeper must know exactly how to react, how to judge the angles in coming out to meet a forward who has broken through on his own.

Too much use of a protective goal area can give a goalkeeper a false sense of security. And while, as an attacking player myself, I'm all in favour of lulling an opposing goalkeeper into a state of vulnerable complacency, I like to know that the keeper in my own team is kept as sharp as possible thanks to the right balance of work in training.

The ball

Competitive five-a-side football means playing with a size four ball, though the Americans in their indoor six-a-side game use the full-size variety.

In outdoor informal five-a-side work I would always favour using the ball you use for eleven-a-side. That means standard size for senior players, but of course the smaller size for youngsters.

I've always been a little disturbed in official five-a-side tournaments at switching to the smaller ball. I appreciate that the goals and the pitch are smaller, but it does seem like a marble and you can't work with it as with a standard ball. You can't bend the ball in the same way nor shoot with the same power.

So the lesson is clear: if you're in organised five-a-side tournaments, make sure you are comfortable with the

One-to-one situation in five-a-side – but stay out of that goal area!

31

smaller ball. That could make all the difference at the start of your first game, especially if your opponents make a better start because they have done their practical homework.

However, if your five-a-side involvement is part of preparation for eleven-a-side competition, then don't waste your money on the smaller ball!

Match duration

Organised five-a-side consists of two halves of six minutes each, with two extra-time periods of two minutes each if the scores are still level. But the Football League's Soccer Six is played on the basis of two halves of ten minutes each, with no provision for extra time.

As for the Americans, you can trust them to be bigger, if not better. The NASL indoor rules lay down that a match there shall last four quarters of fifteen minutes. Cynics may say that this a spin-off from American gridiron football or just so that television can take advantage of more advertising breaks.

But it's a fact that five-a-side or six-a-side football is physically extremely demanding. In training with Tottenham I've grown used to playing about twenty minutes each half and we all come off very tired at the final whistle!

The reason is obvious: with nothing like the number of stoppages for free kicks, throw-ins, corners − yes, and injuries − the mini game can be virtually perpetual motion with each player having to cover a lot of ground and involve himself in both defence and attack to a larger extent than in a conventional game. When you think about it, the ball isn't in play for a lot longer than twenty minutes each half in a normal League or Cup game, so don't be deceived by the apparently limited timing of mini football.

Beware the demands, in particular, of the indoor game. Everyone in five-a-side football wants the ball and is involved in chasing forward, chasing back, closing men down and trying to win the ball. But the fact of working so close to everybody else, allied to all the turning, stopping, twisting and accelerating involved means there is an injury risk − particularly in the gymnasium or on a concrete surface. You stand to collect more than a few minor bruises, too. I've known First Division players put out of the next Saturday's game because of an injury suffered in a five-a-side.

The ankles, in particular, can take a hammering and I would advise anyone involved in five-a-side to seriously consider strapping their ankles. In the case of the many players who have collected a few ankle knocks over the years that is all the more important. It can make all the difference between walking off at the final whistle and hobbling off much earlier. That, after all, is not helping your team, whether unlimited substitutions are allowed or not.

Dropped ball

Nothing to do with nervous goalkeepers!

The dropped ball is the way a game is restarted in mini football. You might play half-a-dozen First Division games without one referee resorting to a dropped ball, but the more times you see this in five-a-side the better — because that means plenty of goals and plenty of entertainment, both for players and spectators.

In senior soccer, in fact, referees don't like to use the dropped ball. They fear, I think, that it might seem a weakness, signalling to the players that they weren't up with play, and might undermine their authority.

But just as some referees are more ready to admit they were unsighted than others, so referees vary in the way they conduct the bounce-up. Some really do bounce the ball down so it comes up fast, while others just pat the ball down and beat a hasty retreat.

When I was a youngster I remember that we always called up our biggest, strongest player if a dropped ball had been awarded. That was for two reasons: first, because a dropped ball is often followed by a block tackle between the two players; and secondly, because a player involved in a dropped ball can take quite a whack from the opponent's boot, accidentally.

Obviously that danger doesn't arise indoors, where the players aren't using studs but some form of training shoe. However I still prefer it when the referee bounces the ball

with some force. The element of surprise and the need to step back to gain the room to play the ball seems to reduce the chance of getting caught by a stray boot and also provides a better opportunity for getting the ball back into play effectively.

Opposite: Restarting play with a dropped ball.

Head height

Organising five-a-side demands that the ball be kept below head height and though this is not strictly necessary for training work, it is valuable in developing technique.

Wherever you play, in whatever standard of football, to increase your own enjoyment of the game you need to obtain a basic mastery of the ball. And that means the sort of control to keep the ball low whether in passing over long and short distances or in shooting.

More specifically the head height rule works in mini football to increase the football awareness of defenders. In five-a-side play the goalkeeper can distribute the ball only by bowling it out, underarm. The easy option of kicking the

Goalkeepers must roll the ball out underarm.

ball downfield over the tops of everyone's heads is ruled out.
Therefore, defenders have to learn how to move and position
themselves and escape markers to be free to receive the ball
and move it on. Learning a positive approach to the game in
this way and for this reason can also help the defender to
understand his defensive role and more effectively cover and
shadow his immediate attacking rival.

Fouls and misconduct

Five-a-side is a non-contact version of football in its
competitive form. For example, a shoulder charge which
would be accepted in the middle of Wembley Stadium would
incur a direct free kick if repeated indoors at Wembley
Arena.

Obstruction is an offence in both codes, but one infringement peculiar to mini football relates to unauthorised entry
of an outfield player into the goalkeeper's area.

If an attacking player is to blame then the punishment is
a direct free kick at the point of entry into the goalkeeper's
area. However, if the referee decides that a defending player
deliberately encroached in the attempt to play the ball, then
that's a penalty.

Although the mini game is officially a non-contact form of
football, there are bound to be occasional accidents. One of
the most unnerving is when a player turns to take a rebound
off the perimeter only to be virtually bowled over by another
player rushing in past him. In the gymnasium, where the
head height rule hasn't applied, I have frequently seen a
goalkeeper – jumping to catch a rebound from the wall
above his goal – upset by a couple of forwards clattering in
over his shoulders while he was unsighted.

I have also – and I think it's only fair that coaches,
teachers and would-be officials should be warned – seen
more than a few instances of sheer bad temper break the
surface. Feelings can run very high when you are playing on
top of one another in a confined space. In a conventional
match two players might catch each other, but then not
come into contact for another five or ten minutes because of
their positions or the flow of the play. In five-a-side there is
no automatic, built-in cooling-off period.

Kevin Bond is sent for two minutes in the sin bin at the National Exhibition Centre.

Sin bin

This idea, borrowed from ice hockey, has been used successfully in six-a-side events. It provides just that cooling-off facility not available to players battling it out at close quarters in five-a-sides.

The Football League's Soccer Six rules lay down that a player should be sent into the sin bin for two minutes for persistent fouling, dissent, ungentlemanly conduct, time-wasting, encroaching at free kicks and – an ingenious one – giving a goalkeeper a return back pass. These offences also incur an indirect free kick.

The sin bin does not replace the referee's power to permanently send off a player. That is still the ultimate

penalty for violent conduct, serious foul play, using foul or abusive language and persistent foul play by a man who has already spent time in the sin bin.

Just in case the fans didn't get the message!

In the context of organised indoor competition, I think the sin bin has a part to play. It adds to the entertainment and the novelty of the game and leaves the players in no doubt that they must try their hardest not to infringe the rules.

But whether the sin bin approach could work in the conventional game, I doubt. The muscle injury risks would be enormous with players constantly trotting off, getting cold, having to warm up again – to say nothing of the disruption to the flow of play. In mini football there are few interruptions in play. But in the conventional game, with corners, free kicks and throw-ins, I think we have enough already.

Throw-ins

The FA's five-a-side rules state baldly that 'there are no goal kicks, corners or throw-ins.'

That may be right for the competitive mini match in an indoor arena with a rebound wall. But it's not much in the way of guidance if you count five-a-side football as part of an outdoor training session. In these circumstances some throw-in/corner kick ruling is essential or the game and players will disappear over some distant hill!

So I would suggest varying the approach to restarting the game in these situations with a standard throw-in, or a hand-on. Using a normal throw-in is valuable practice regarding off-the-ball movement and decoy runs.

As for the hand-on, that involves placing the ball down and quickly chipping or clipping it forward — depending on whether you are applying a head height rule. That way a team gains extra practice with free kicks.

Penalties

A mini football tournament being played over one or two nights can't afford any drawn games and I believe that a penalty shoot-out is the best way to decide matters because it is a form of the game which players and fans alike understand.

The drama is also immense. You have only to recall the penalty contest between France and West Germany at the 1982 World Cup finals to know that. More than a dozen of the game's finest players were literally put on the spot, with a place in the Final itself at stake. Not every penalty shoot-out carries such significance, but the format has an inbuilt drama which is the same whether at the end of a conventional game or a five or six-a-side match.

Also, though the penalty distances are shorter and the goals smaller, the kicking technique doesn't vary. I take a five-a-side penalty in exactly the same way as I took the kick which won the 1982 FA Cup Final replay for Tottenham against Queen's Park Rangers.

Every player has his own approach or ritual. In my case, I

aim to clear my mind of everything else so that I can be positive about the task in hand. I always look at the goalkeeper beforehand and also towards one corner of the net – though I don't always hit the ball in that direction. Then I like to place the ball and get on with the job. When you are running up you don't really see the goalkeeper. Maybe out of the corner of your eye, but nothing like enough to influence which way you hit the ball.

Scoring from the penalty spot.

Opposite: Not even England goal-keeper Peter Shilton can do anything about this penalty.

The only difference between conventional and five-a-side football is the size of the goal itself, which means that whereas you may get away with mis-hitting a penalty just up under the bar in a League game, make the same mistake in fives and the ball's in the crowd!

As for the goalkeeper, he's in the same enviable position whether the game is indoors or out, whether the goals are scaled-down or full size. If he is beaten, no one will blame him — but if he pulls off the save then he's a hero!

4

Techniques and Training

Good technique is essential in any form of football. That might seem an obvious comment, but I believe that even in the professional game we pay too little attention to technique in the concentration on tactics and the more demanding coaching ideas and exercises.

But, first, what do I mean by technique? It's a forbidding word, perhaps, for a simple subject: the art of controlling and using a football. The better your technique, the more effective a player you become.

The Brazilians are without a doubt the most gifted players in the world when it comes to technical ability. It is more than coincidence that they were the first nation to win the World Cup three times. If you read about the childhood days of Pelé, Garrincha, or Zico, you will be struck by a common factor: they spent hours playing football. And if there were no friends to form a team then they kicked the ball against a wall, or the paving stones, to develop their control.

Of course, as kids they didn't realise the effect of what they were up to. But how all that practice paid off!

The better your technique, the better you will play and the better you will play — in particular — in five-a-side football. The pitch and player restrictions place, as we have seen, a great emphasis on individual skill, on the ability to beat an opponent and create the one-man advantage so valuable in attacking goal.

It's not my intention to go right back to basics on control and use of the ball (you can find that in the dozens of ordinary coaching manuals around), but I am concerned to suggest practical ways in which to improve your ability to play the game — and prepare for it. So here I shall pinpoint those key areas in which the five-a-side footballer must be proficient to make the most of his ability and enthusiasm.

Key to accuracy, passing with the inside of the foot.

Passing the ball

This may appear almost too obvious a starting point. But as much skill is involved in passing the ball as in holding it — in this case the skill being both mental and physical.

To pass the ball accurately and effectively you have to be aware — aware of when to make the pass, aware of your team-mates, aware of your opponents. Over the years a succession of labels have been applied to this mental skill — one such was 'peripheral vision'. But it all adds up to the same thing: being alive to what is happening in the game around you.

The correct and full control of the ball are essential, but even then your pass can go astray. And how will you make the pass? The traditional method is by using the inside of the foot and guiding the ball on its course either to the feet of a team-mate, or into an open space for him to run on to it.

But you can also gain a split-second advantage over your direct opponents if you can perfect and use the pass with the outside of the foot. This is as easily carried out as it sounds, but depends on a strong ankle since it is a disguised late movement which is hard for an opponent to read and anticipate.

In football half a second can make the vital difference between sending a forward clear for a crack at goal or enduring the frustration of seeing him caught offside.

Either way, passing with the inside or outside of the foot, remember: keep your head up and your head steady. And when you have decided to make your pass, hit the ball quickly and firmly. Be decisive. There's nothing more dangerous than a player caught in two minds when he is about to release the ball. More often than not an opponent intercepts and that fatal hesitation has put your defence under pressure.

In five-a-side football, when you may often be the last line of defence in front of the goalkeeper, inaccurate passing is punished even more readily than outdoors. In five-a-side it may not be as far to your opponents' goal – but it's not as far to your own, either. Indecision could prove fatal.

Shooting

As with passing the ball in five-a-side, where there's no point in recommending the use of the chip because of ball height restrictions, similarly, in shooting, it's no good thinking about aiming for the top corner. Your shot will fly into the crowd and your team will be penalised.

But just as the extra concentration on accuracy in five-a-side passing can be valuable when transferred to the eleven-a-side, so in shooting the necessary indoor concentration on keeping the ball low is no handicap on the full-size pitch.

As there are two basic passing methods, so there are two basic methods of shooting.

Power comes from the instep, but accuracy comes from the inside of the foot. Obviously the player will decide in a split-second which method to apply when the ball lands at his feet in front of goal – so confidence in being able to hit a shot both ways is essential.

If the ball comes your way twenty yards out and a shot is possible then the instep will usually be the favourite to provide the power which beats the goalkeeper's anticipation. On the other hand, closer to goal and with perhaps a little more time the inside of the foot is more deadly. Misused power can often see the ball flying off in the wrong direction. For sureness of touch, the inside of the foot has plenty of advantages. That's how I prefer to shoot – to 'pass the ball into the net', as some coaches call it.

The outside of the foot can also be used for shooting, but because this is generally the least powerful method, you won't find many goals scored that way. The aim in shooting

Following through after a shot with the outside of the foot.

is to get the ball into the net with the highest degree of power, accuracy and speed. By using the outside of the foot, giving the goalkeeper less warning and less chance to anticipate, it is possible to further confuse him by 'bending' the shot.

But, because your head isn't naturally over the ball it requires a great deal of practice indeed to hit it hard with the outside of the foot *and* keep it low.

Practices

The aim of training, with the ball or without it, is to help the player become more effective out on the pitch. It is not an end in itself.

As we have said, the basic need is for good technique — ball control. One of the simplest practice methods (see Fig 1) is for two players to hit the ball to and fro from varying distances, up to a maximum of twenty yards. The plan is simple: one player makes the pass, the other controls the ball either by trapping it with the sole of the foot or 'cushioning' it with the inside of the foot. Once the ball is dead he returns the pass.

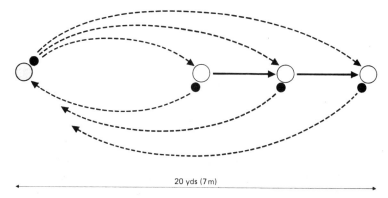

20 yds (7 m)

Fig 1: Passing practise over varied distances.

This need not become monotonous while the players alter the gap between them and interrupt the static exercise with a running-and-passing exercise over twenty yards. After all, much of the passing of a ball during a game — both giving and receiving — takes place while players are on the move.

The exercise can be futher varied by placing a series of obstacles between the players (see Fig 2). The ball must then be passed with an increased awareness of timing and touch to keep it in play. This is a particularly useful preparation for the five-a-side game when the permanent proximity of opposing players means that the wall pass, so necessary to cut out an opponent, is in high demand.

Even footballs will do as obstacles to
help improve your ball control.

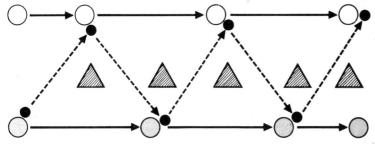

Fig 2: Obstacle passing with two players on the move.

But of course you don't need a partner to practise ball control. As long as you have a football and a wall of some sort you can work out on your own — as all the great players did in their day.

Boys often play with a tennis ball, which has plenty of advantages in terms of establishing deftness of control and concentration, but there's no substitute for the real thing. Only a ball of the right size and weight should be used where possible so that a player's balance and timing is developed correctly. And in preparing for five-a-side football that means, of course, using the smaller-size ball in training.

You also need to master control of the ball with both feet — or get as near to that as possible. There have been some great 'one-footed' players in the history of the game — Hungary's Ferenc Puskas and today Argentina's Diego Maradona — but they have been the exceptions which prove the rule. To progress and make the most of your general ability you need to be able to control and hit the ball with both right and left feet.

I can't stress that enough. I'm fortunate because I can do that. If I'm asked which is my stronger foot, I can't answer — I believe I can hit the ball equally well with either. But that doesn't apply to most players. In fact, I would say that perhaps as many as ninety-five per cent of First Division players are basically one-footed.

This is an aspect of the game in Britain to which not enough attention is paid. In fact we don't work hard enough on technique in general. Why not? I don't know. What I do know is that for successful five-a-side there is no substitute for a sound technique. And in developing technique there is

not substitute for hard, although enjoyable, work.

Passing and shooting are essential skills which demand control of a ball. But because the old adage that the ball should run faster than the player remains true, it doesn't mean that the skills of dribbling are losing their value.

Most of us have read about how Sir Stanley Matthews was nicknamed the Wizard of Dribble — slipping down the right wing as if the ball was tied to his bootlaces. More recently

my hero George Best possessed magical individual talent to
go past one man after another without ever having to
stretch to keep the ball at his feet. Watch the South
Americans – and the Brazilians above all – to see such
control today.

As I have said, that ability is a product both of natural
talent and also of hard work. So here are some exercises
which can be used enjoyably to develop those skills.

Two against two

Mark out a pitch of about 20 yards in length but only a few yards wider than the five-a-side goals. Then play two against two with goalkeepers in place. This exercise is enjoyable because it involves actual play, but it is also valuable for fitness and stamina and encourages both sharp movement off the ball and an emphasis on the techniques in beating your marker.

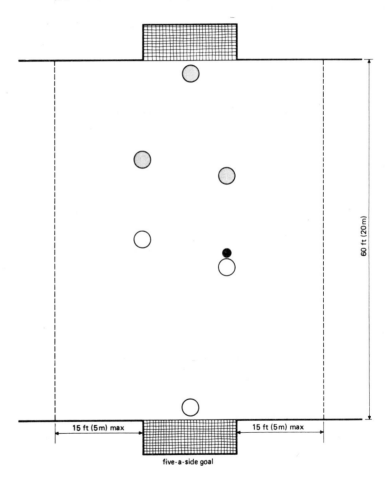

Fig 3: Two against two – with goalkeepers – on a restricted pitch.

Five against two

Form a grid with five players standing in a rectangle. Then put two players in the middle whose challenge is to cut out the one – or two – touch passes between the perimeter players.

This exercise is valuable both for instant control and for awareness and is particularly popular in West Germany. A string of World Cup, European Championship and European club successes over the past decade can't be a bad recommendation!

Again this is an exercise which involves plenty of movement and can be clearly related to match situations.

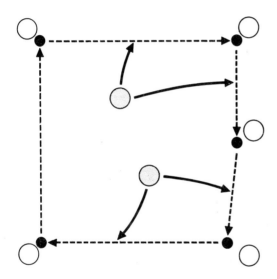

Fig 4: Interception exercise.

'Skittles'

This exercise is to improve dribbling and close continuous control and is perhaps the first training exercise most people remember from their days out on the football pitch at school.

Set out a line of spare footballs, skittles, cones, or any other markers (even dustbins will do!) and dribble in and out between them. This can become boring for one person if repeated too frequently, but it's amazing how much enthusi-

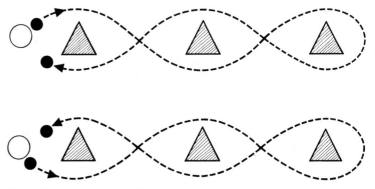

Fig 5: Ball control competition.

asm can be whipped up by adding a competitive edge —
timing players against each other, for instance.

Clearly, the better and tighter the control, the faster the
player can snake between the obstacles and return to base.

Goalkeeping

A goalkeeper in any form of the game relies on secure
handling and sharp reflexes. To what extent you can carry
out one of the most useful 'pressure' exercises depends on
how many footballs you have to spare!

Throw a line of five or six players across the face of the
goal area at varying distances and angles from the keeper.
Have the shooters number off and then the coach (or one of
the players) should call out the numbers in any sequence he
likes.

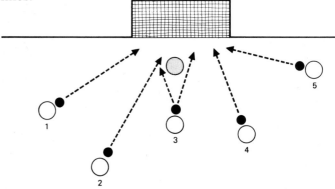

Fig 6: Goalkeeping reflex practice.

Keeping the shot low.

As he calls a player's number so that player shoots for goal and the moment the goalkeeper has saved (or not!) then the coach should be calling another player's number to have a crack from another angle.

You can't keep it going for too long, but a number of short sharp stints can do wonders for a goalkeeper's reflexes – even if you might need to be careful not to undermine his confidence. And remember, in the five-a-side context, all those shots must be kept low.

This chapter has been almost entirely concerned with direct, match-related skills. But clearly the five-a-side footballer has to maintain a reasonable level of fitness to be in condition for the short concentrated bursts of the game.

General fitness is not the aim. It's not much good relying on jogging, for example, to prepare for a football match. The businessman who sits in his office all day will certainly benefit from jogging first thing in the morning; it provides the sort of exercise necessary to maintain a healthy body and mind. But that's not much use of a footballer. Football is a running game. It's about short dashes, about 30- and 40-yard sprints and these are the demands on which a player should base his training.

There has been plenty in the newspapers about managers taking players for long treks over the sand dunes or indulging in gruelling pre-season cross-country work. But that is related to general stamina. Once the season is under way what is important is relating training to match play.

Each player is different and needs an individual approach. For example, some Tottenham players are keen on weights work. But I find this most useful only in building up the muscles again after an injury. Too much weights work in midweek and I feel sluggish on a match day – and correct training should aim to bring you to the kick-off in relaxed but peak condition.

Everyone has to find his own level. If you watch a Brazilian team in training you will see that their work-outs involve what are virtually dance routines. That's fine for a Brazilian who has an inbuilt poise and suppleness. But I think the British player needs something a little more practical – whatever Bobby Gould started at Coventry with ballet instruction!

Opposite: Working out with the weights in the Tottenham gymnasium.

58

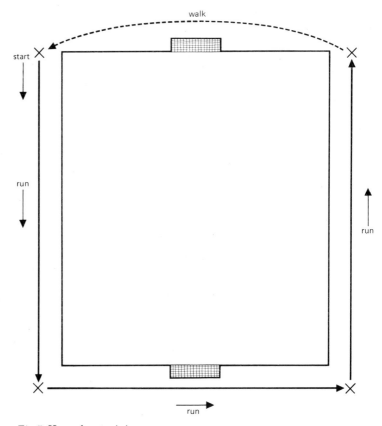

Fig 7: Horseshoe training run.

A simple example of what I mean is the 'horseshoe' exercise (see Fig. 7). This involves simply running or sprinting round three sides of a pitch (long–short–long) and then taking a 'rest' as you walk the fourth (short) side before breaking into a run again.

The old idea that mindless lapping of the pitch was the best training exercise has, thankfully, gone out of the window. So has the idea that if you kept the players without a football in midweek it would make them the more hungry for it come match-day.

I'll make the point again: training must be related to the game. You can work out plenty more exercises of your own both to develop technique and fitness levels. But always ask yourself the key question: is this a positive help to my game?

5

Getting the Tactics Right

There are plenty of fans — and not a few players and managers! — who believe that tactics are a form of numbers game.

I suppose it was Brazil who started it. When they won the 1958 World Cup in Sweden with a formation which was new to Europe (though at least a decade old in South America) 'Tactics' became the game's most popular word. The Brazilian style was called 4–2–4, with four men spread across the back, two in midfield and four up front. Four years later in the World Cup in Chile they pulled one front man back into midfield and we were regaled with 4–3–3. Then Sir Alf Ramsey built England's so called 'wingless wonders' who won the 1966 World Cup with a figuration which was something like 4–4–2. At the 1978 World Cup the Dutch team who reached the final used a scheme created by their coach, Ernst Happel, which was nicknamed 'The Fog', and was described as 3–5–2. And that was just about all the man in the street — or on the terraces — was told about tactics. The variation in numbers blinded many people to the fact that tactics are all about organisation and getting the best out of the players available.

Obviously, in five-a-side or six-a-side the concept of the game means that there are none of these numbers games. I am not going to preach a 1–1–3 system or 1–3–1. As far as I am concerned, as is anyone who has played a lot of five-a-side, this is one version of football in which set positions go out of the window.

The goalkeeper is an obvious exception. He can't go racing all over the pitch. But everyone else generally has to fulfil the role of defender, midfield or attacker depending on the state of the game and the problems or gaps created by the opposition. Once the other team get the ball, everyone's

Fig 8: Lone Attacker: The value of leaving one man permanently in attack – cancelling out an opponent who has to stay with him rather than join his own team's attack.

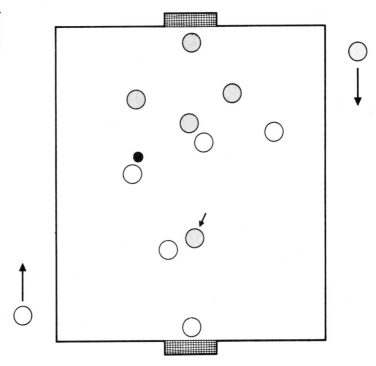

priority is to get goal-side. Then start looking around to pick up attacking players.

The only circumstances in which this can be varied is in six-a-side football, where the rules stipulate that one player must remain upfield at all times. That is a situation worth experiencing within five-a-side too, although. If you instruct one player to remain upfield, no matter how the opposition are pressing forward, the chances are that one of their players will drop back to mark him and be effectively cancelled out. That in turn puts more pressure on their attackers and assists the defending team. Also, if all their players should come forward and then lose possession, one accurate through–pass can send your own lone striker clear on his own to go through and have a crack at goal.

Some people might say that these are the tactics of caution and counter-attack which the Italians have taught us. But there are plenty of accounts in football's history books of Arsenal using the same ideas in the 1930s when Herbert Chapman introduced the stopper centre-half.

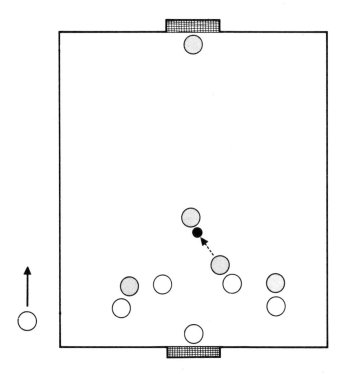

Fig 9: The Anchor Man: The value of having an anchor man just behind the main thrust of attack.

Tactics, as we've said, are all about organisation. For example, consider this idea to make the most of your players and your possession of the ball: create an 'anchor man'. He isn't, as you might suppose, a pivot in midfield, but a player detailed to hang back from the main body of the team on the attack. It means that if an attacker is under pressure on the ball he always has the option of playing the ball back to the anchor man. The value of that is clear. When the opposition are well-drilled enough to fall back *en masse* as you attack, then the anchor man is presented with an extra five or ten yards space in which to size up the attacking options and create an opening somewhere else. It takes some practice and it takes an intelligent player who can use his head as well as his feet, and read the game well. But once the scheme has been perfected, then a team's effectiveness can be multiplied. And that multiplication can be demonstrated in goals.

But you will never get goals without shooting. That's an elementary lesson which many teams — plenty of international and League teams as well! − appear to forget. The Dutch team who finished runners-up in the 1978 World Cup demonstrated the point perfectly: they reckoned that the more shots they had at goal − from whatever distance − the more they would score. Players such as Arie Haan scored some spectacular long-range goals because no one was afraid to have a go and in five-a-side the opportunity arises more often because of the shortened pitch.

What counts in shooting is not only the power and direction of the shot, but the element of surprise. An experienced goalkeeper learns to judge where a shot is going by the manner in which a forward prepares to strike the ball. But the snap-shot, the shot from beyond a crowd of players, and the shot from an acute angle can often beat a goalkeeper more by surprise than anything else.

Five-a-side tournaments have built a reputation for entertainment because of the number of goals and the frequency of the goal attempts.

Also, the team prepared to shoot hard and often, save their own energy, because they are not perpetually running around exchanging a string of stamina-sapping passes merely keeping possession and making no positive progress.

Those are some key thoughts on attacking. But what about defending? Five-a-side or six-a-side football demands a high level of skill from defenders. The reduced number of players per team means that individual flair and techniques is all the more significant. And a defender must be able to deal with the most skilled forward without always being pressured into giving away free kicks and penalties.

Part of the art of defending is experience: knowing when to make the tackle and when to hold off. In five-a-side football a defender is always aware of the fact that there is precious little cover behind him. If an attacker gets past, then the next line of defence is the goalkeeper! There's no sweeper permanently assigned to patrol the goal area. In a game with only five players per team, that would be a waste of a man.

For a player who fills a defensive role in a standard eleven-a-side team, the five-a-side game can open new horizons. As we have seen, there are no fixed positions. If your team has the ball you are all attackers, whether your normal position is outside right or left back.

Waiting for the tackle.

The mobility and movement allowed in the five-a-side game is part of the team pattern. It's not a free-for-all, or at least is shouldn't be. And the key method for ensuring that each player knows what everyone else is up to is through shouting.

Communication is vital in every walk of life, at home or in industry. And that makes it all the more amazing that many school teachers running football matches ban their young players from shouting. I suffered some of that strange régime at school and I am still trying to understand the reasons behind it. Shouting is an important part of the game. If you went along to a training match you would probably be amazed at the amount of shouting.

Some years ago Sir Stanley Rous, then president of FIFA, spoke out. He said there was too much shouting in the game. That surprised me, too – that a man of his standing and experience in football apparently failed to appreciate the need. After all, when you play in front of crowds of forty thousand regularly, it's hard to make yourself heard over five or ten yards. any communication *has* to be shouted.

To put it in obvious terms: each player has to be the eyes and ears of the man on the ball. He may not know that an opponent is closing in on the blind side or that a team-mate is ready to move into position for a clear run at goal. He cannot know and cannot make the best use of his ability unless someone else tells him.

In defence it's imperative for a goalkeeper to shout his intensions whether in five-a-side or eleven-a-side football. Is he going to stay on his line or come out for a cross? His fellow defenders cannot know unless he tells them and in the most decisive terms.

Also defenders seeing two forwards working a cross-over need a quick word to agree whether to follow their assigned player, or stand their ground and pick up the man coming their way.

All by shouting. That is part of the necessary organisation of a team while the game is in progress. And organisation is what tactics are all about.

7

It's Nothing New

The advent of rapid-action, televised six-a-side football has been greeted in the last couple of years as a revolutionary step forward for the game as a whole. But a brief look back over the history of mini football will soon show that there's really nothing new under the sun.

In April 1940, the early days of the second world war, Brentford were sounding out other London clubs with plans for a six-a-side knock-out tournament. Manager Harry Curtis said at the time: 'My proposal is that eight teams should compete in games of seven minutes each way. The whole competition could be over in three hours. If sufficient clubs are interested there could be more than one tournament. . .'

Most people in England then had rather more pressing matters on their mind and it was to take more than forty years before Harry Curtis's dream came true — at least where six-a-side soccer was concerned.

The fact is that fives, being a hybrid adaptation of the outdoor game, was viewed with grave suspicion by the football authorities for years and an early attempt to launch a tournament at Wembley, in the autumn of 1949, found players and officials at loggerheads.

This was one of the first issues, in fact, over which the players' union, the Professional Footballers' Association, flexed its muscles — an exercise which led ultimately to the revolt which saw to the abolition of the maximum wage, freedom of contract and a respected place for players' leaders around the game's conference tables.

But long after the players had brought about a measure of industrial democracy to the game, five-a-side competiton had taken off. In 1951 the London Evening Standard organised a London professional championship, played initially at Harringay, and within two years it was pulling in nearly ten thousand fans. One of the early stars was the current England manager Bobby Robson. When Fulham won the 1953 competition he scored a hat-trick against Charlton in the semi-final and two more goals in a 4—1 win over West Ham in the final. Fulham's entertaining line-up also included Johnny Haynes, and the captain was Jimmy Hill, who remarked afterwards: 'Our kind of football works perfectly on an indoor surface. I only wish it did as well on the heavier grounds outdoors!'

The crowd-pulling potential of five-a-side football was now obvious and it was quickly recognised that it could be increased even further by lining up some of the game's most famous names. In 1959 a tournament to benefit the National Sports Development fund was organised with the promise of a turn-out by the likes of Stanley Matthews, Tom Finney, Billy Wright, Danny Blanchflower and Johnny Haynes. But much of the steam went out of the venture when the Football League advised their clubs to refuse consent to any players wishing to take part. League president Joe Richards said: 'It is in the clubs' interests that we should take this action.'

It was to be another twenty-five years before the League realised that in a world where the various forms of sporting recreation are becoming ever more eager rivals, football would *need* the sort of promotion such top-line mini tournaments could bring.

Meanwhile the London five-a-side tournament continued its successful path, with not a little thanks to West Ham's 1966 World Cup-winners. The Hammers, beaten three times in previous finals, eventually collected the trophy in 1967. Their team was made up of Bobby Moore, Martin Peters, Geoff Hurst, Ron Boyce and goalkeeper Colin Mackleworth. Hurst — England's hat-trick hero against West Germany in the World Cup Final — scored two more triples at the Wembley indoor arena against both Queen's Park Rangers and then Arsenal in the final.

Ten years after the Football League had frowned on the idea of senior internationals providing the all-star element for such indoor tournaments, the clubs themselves had quietly seen the light. And few five-a-side teams have ever been as star-studded at the squad Manchester United announced for the third edition of the new *Daily Express*

National Championships in 1970. Manager Wilf McGuinness selected Alex Stepney, David Sadler, Bobby Charlton, Denis Law and George Best, and then commented modestly: 'George is pretty special when it comes to five-a-side football. The game is tailor-made for his skill. I don't believe in predictions but I think it's fair to suggest that our team will be worth watching!' United duly carried off the trophy.

Five-a-side football had developed from being a regional event, which would draw committed fans to follow their teams, to an accepted entertainment. Its value for introducing youngsters to the game was emphasised when the *Daily Express* backed an under-18 championship.

That didn't mean the end of the paper's senior National Championship involvement. This became an established part of the football calendar and it was in the 1970s that I found my five-a-side feet in the Wembley finals. Tottenham beat Ipswich on penalties in the 1972 final, but we went out

Action at Wembley Arena in the 1984 London five-a-side.

Orient beat us in the *Daily Express* National five-a-side final in November 1974. The winners celebrate with Lady Aitken.

to eventual winners Derby in the first round the following year. In 1974 Orient beat us in the final, as did Wolves in 1975. But whatever the results I always found the competition exhilerating and the atmosphere electric.

The results of these major tournaments were often pointers to trends in the conventional outdoor game. For example, when Aston Villa collected the *Express* trophy in November 1980, their skipper on the night, Kenny Swain, said: 'This is the first of many honours we expect to pick up this season. . .' But even Kenny, in all his wildest dreams, would probably not have expected that six months later Villa would become Football League champions and go on the next season to land the European Cup as well!

It was then that Scotland Yard got in on the act,

launching a huge five-a-side youth tournament as part of the softly-softly fight against crime. The then Metropolitan Police Commissioner, Sir David McNee, decided that such a tournament could achieve the two-fold effect of keeping some of the jobless youngsters occupied, and also helping relations between London's youth and the police in general. My England colleague Trevor Brooking, whose brother was a police inspector, helped promote the tournament which is just about the biggest of its kind in the world with around thirty thousand youngsters aged between ten and eighteen taking part.

Mind you, police involvement may be considered long overdue after one or two minor altercations I remember in the five-a-side world. Stan Bowles staged a walk-out near

England's Trevor Brooking and the Met. Police's Sir Kenneth Newman launch the fourth of their youth five-a-side tournaments.

71

the end of Spurs' Wembley semi-final against QPR in 1974 and two years later my future Tottenham team-mate, Garth Crooks, was furious at being 'credited' with a controversial and decisive own goal when Wolves beat Stoke to the trophy.

But the development of the indoor game hasn't taken place only in Britain. A European veterans' five-a-side was organised at Meadowbank, Edinburgh, in 1971 with Hungary's Nandor Hidegkuti among the squad. Attempts were made to launch a World Indoor Championship circus a couple of years later — that fell foul of player insurance snags. But across Europe the footballers of Switzerland, Austria and West Germany were taking advantage of their weather-enforced winter breaks to keep fit and sharp with indoor competition, and in the United States the concept caught on faster than anywhere.

Ironically it was a Soviet team who provided the catalyst for the Americans: TSKA of Moscow, the Red Army club. during a North American tour they played an indoor game at the Spectrum arena in Philadelphia . . . and the ecstatic response from the fans convinced a Washington lawyer, Earl Foreman, that this version of soccer might catch on more readily than the eleven-a-side outdoor version.

On 10 November 1977 the Major Indoor Soccer League was launched when Foreman, co-founder Ed Tepper and representatives of nine major indoor arenas met in New York. A 'high-powered, fast-paced action contest . . . played in luxurious surroundings' was their aim, and so successful was the product that it wasn't long before the outdoor North American Soccer League were following suit with their own indoor competition.

An expatriate Yugoslav from Hajduk Split, known at home as Slavissa Zungul but Americanised as Steve Zungul, quickly became the star performer, rattling in goal after goal in this six-a-side package which streamlined the old five-a-side rules and added a sin bin and various other facets to suit the American public's taste for instant-action sport. Star players were soon earning around £70,000 a season and such was the reaction to this development of the indoor game that one-time England and QPR star Rodney Marsh commented: 'It looks more and more as if the future of football in America will be indoors.'

With financial problems becoming ever more pressing, it was no wonder that the English League clubs took up the idea. The result was the then Atari-sponsored Soccer Six, launched at the National Exhibition Centre, Birmingham, in January 1983. There was £25,000 in prize money at stake and, while the players took a while to adjust to the strange new format, they still gave the notably hooligan-free spectators their money's worth. Birmingham beat Ipswich 6—4 in the final and, together with Everton, Arsenal, Nottingham Forest, Southampton, Swansea and Manchester City, did enough to suggest that there is plenty of scope for Soccer Six in the future. There were, of course, some mixed views about the style of the game and the additional rules and pitch markings. But without experimentation there can never be progress.

The six-a-side revolution moves to Scotland with the Tennent Caledonian Breweries tournament at Falkirk.

Because of our tight schedule Tottenham couldn't take part in the Birmingham tournament but I watched the television highlights avidly — as, I'm sure, did millions of others who love their football.

The key to the game's future — indoors or outdoors — is entertainment. It is a professional business and if the public don't like what they see, then they have a perfect right to stay away. Any way to encourage entertaining football, invention and adventure in the game deserves encouragement. The spread and growth of organised five and six-a-side football is a development all those in the outdoor game should welcome.

I am not suggesting that the mini game will one day take over from the eleven-a-side version. But if the attitudes can be carried over — at least at professional level — then, thanks to television, so the public at large will see football's image improving.

West Ham, winners of the 1984 five-a-side final at Wembley Arena with the *Standard* London Five-a-Side Championship trophy.

Appendix 1

From the FA Handbook:
Six-a-Side Football

1. The Laws of the Game of Association Football shall apply with the exceptions of Laws 3, 7 and 11.

2. Eight players may be nominated from whom six players shall be chosen to form a team. The game shall be played by two teams each consisting of not more than six players, one of whom shall be the goalkeeper. One of the other players may change places with the goalkeeper during the match provided that notice is given to the Referee before such change is made.

3. During the game only one substitution may be made in the case of injury.

4. There will be no offside.

5. In the event of a match being drawn at full time, it will be decided on the basis of the number of corners gained by each side. If the match is still undecided, play will continue for a further period of six minutes, three minutes each way.

6. The duration of a six-a-side game shall not exceed two equal periods of ten minutes, except in circumstances covered by 5 above. Allowance may be made in either period for time lost through accident or other cause, the amount of which shall be a matter for the discretion of the referee. The interval shall not exceed five minutes.

7. The referee shall be the sole arbiter on points of dispute and he shall be empowered to interpret the rules governing six-a-side football bearing in mind the best interest of all parties concerned.

Five-a-Side Football

Rules: Except where other provisions in these rules are made, the rules of Association Football apply. (Each rule is numbered to correspond with the appropriate Laws of the Game.) These rules are for guidance only and not mandatory. Five-a-side Football may be played or refereed by either men or women. Mixed matches are not permitted.

1. Playing area: Five-a-side Football may be played in an enclosed area indoors or out of doors. The following dimensions are recommended, maximum length 120 ft (36 m), minimum 100 ft (30 m), maximum width 90 ft (28 m), minimum 60 ft (18.5 m).

(a) *Centre Mark:* A suitable area should be made in the exact centre of the playing area on which the ball is dropped to commence a game. The centre spot should be surrounded by a circle 3 ft (1 m) in radius.

(b) *Goal Area:* A semi-circle of 25 ft (7.5 m) radius shall be drawn from the centre of each goal line. The extremities of these semi-circles should reach the wall or barricade regardless of whether or not the goal posts encroach on the the field of play.

(c) *Penalty Mark:* A penalty mark should be placed at a point 20 ft (6 m) from the centre of each goal.

(d) *Goal:* The goals shall be 16 ft (5 m) long by 4 ft (1.2 m) high.

2. The Ball: The ball used shall be a five-a-side ball size four.

3. Number of Players:

(a) The match shall be played by two teams each consisting of not more than five players, one of whom shall be the goalkeeper.

(b) One substitute per team shall be permitted at any time during a game. (Subject to conditions set out in the Laws of the Game.)

(c) Any of the other players may change places with the goalkeeper, provided that the referee is informed before the

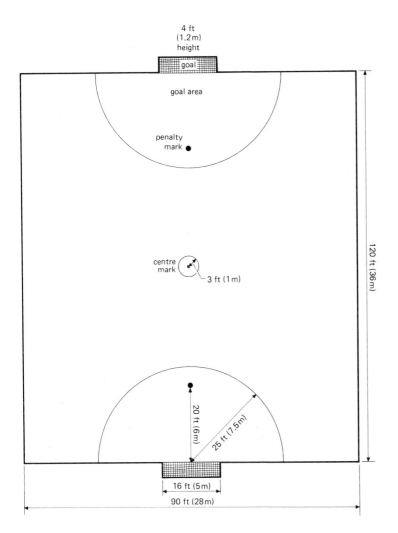

4 ft
(1.2m)
height

goal

goal area

penalty
mark •

centre
mark

3 ft (1 m)

120 ft (36 m)

20 ft (6 m)

25 ft (7.5 m)

16 ft (5 m)

90 ft (28 m)

change is made and provided also that the change is made during a stoppage in the game.

(d) A match should not be considered valid if there are fewer than three players in either of the teams.

4. Players' Equipment:

(a) Four players of the team shall be dressed in uniform shorts and shirts, goalkeepers may wear track suits but the colour of the goalkeepers' dress must be distinguished from that of other players, and the Referee.

(b) *Footwear:* Light footwear shall be worn without rigid or hard soles, bars or studs.

5. Referees: A referee shall be appointed to officiate in each game. He shall have the same powers and duties as laid down in the Laws of the Game.

6. Timekeeper/Scorer: An independent timekeeper/scorer be appointed to assist the referee. This official shall:

(a) record goals scored

(b) act as timekeeper and signify half-time and full-time by an agreed signal

(c) suspend time on the referee's instructions for all stoppages and add that time to the end of each half.

7. Duration of the Game: the duration of the game shall be two equal periods of six minutes. Subject to the following:

(a) Allowance shall be made in either period for time lost through stoppages as decided by the referee and recorded by the timekeeper

(b) Time shall be extended to permit a penalty kick being taken at or after the expiration of the normal period in either half. At half-time the interval shall not exceed two minutes except by consent of the referee.

Drawn games: In the event of scores being level at the end of twelve minutes of play, extra time of two periods of two minutes may be played. If the scores are still level after extra time if played, the rules of the competition shall state the method of ascertaining the winners.

8. Start of Play:

(a) At the beginning of the game the choice of ends shall be decided by the toss of a coin.

(b) Play shall be started by the referee dropping the ball on the centre spot between one player from each side, each of whom shall stand not less from 3 ft (1 m) from the centre mark.

(c) The game shall be re-started in like manner after a goal has been scored.

(d) After any other stoppage the game shall be restarted by the referee dropping the ball at a point nearest to where it was when play was suspended, unless it was in the goalkeeper's possession, when the player shall, at the referee's signal, roll the ball out to re-start the game.

The referee shall not drop the ball within 6 ft (2 m) of the lines marking the goal areas or within 6 ft (2 m) of surrounding walls or barricades.

9. Ball In and Out of Play: The ball shall be in play at all times from the start of the game unless:

(a) the ball rises above head height

(b) the ball has crossed the goal-line or the barricades surrounding the playing area

(c) the timekeeper has given the signal for half or full-time

(d) the game has been stopped by the referee.

Ball above Head Height: The ball must be kept below head height (the referee shall have discretion as to what constitutes 'head height'.) The heading of the ball is allowed provided the aforementioned condition is observed.

Penalty for infringement: Indirect free-kick at the place where the ball was last played (unless the ball was last played by the 'defending goalkeeper' in the goal area, in which case the direct free-kick shall be taken from a point not less than 6 ft (2 m) outside the goal area nearest to where the offence occurred).

If the ball rebounds to above head height from any of the following situations,

(i) From a player who has made no attempt to play the ball

(ii) From a wall, barricade, goalpost, crossbar or other obstruction then the referee will re-start the play by dropping the ball at the point where the rebound occurred. (If this point is within the goal area the ball shall be dropped at a point not less than 6 ft (2 m) outside the goal area nearest to where the rebound occurred.)

Ball out of Play: When the ball goes out of play but below head height, a member of the opposing team shall roll the ball into play. When member of the opposing team puts the ball out of play over the barricade on that player's own goal-line but below head height, the opposing team shall be awarded a roll-in corner. When a member of the attacking team puts the ball out of play over the barricade on the opponents' goal-line, but below head height, the goalkeeper shall roll the ball out. (If the ball drops on the back of the net behind the goal, it shall be regarded as out of play and the game shall be restarted with a roll-out by the goalkeeper.)

10. Scoring: A goal is scored when the whole of the ball crosses the goal-line between the goal posts and under the crossbar provided it has not been thrown, carried or propelled by hand or arm by a player of the attacking side, except in the case of a goalkeeper who is within his own area.

A goal is not allowed if the ball was last played by a player of the attacking side whilst within either goal area. (If the ball is last played by a defending player whilst within either goal area, a goal shall be allowed, unless that player entered the goal area accidentally.)

11. Offside: There is no offside. Players may place themselves in any part of the playing area outside the goal areas.

12. Fouls and Misconduct:

(a) Charging is forbidden and shall be penalised by the awarding of a direct free-kick.

(b) A player who intentionally obstructs an opponent when not playing the ball shall be penalised by the award of an indirect free kick.

A player who is sent off shall not be allowed to taken any further part in the competition on that day, nor in subsequent rounds until permission is given by the Committee governing the competition. The referee must report cases of misconduct within two days (Sundays not included) to the Sanctioning Association.

No substitute is allowed for a player dismissed from the playing area for misconduct during the game in which the offence occurred, but a substitute may be played in any ensuing games.

13. Free-kick: When a player is taking a direct or indirect free-kick, all of the opposing players shall be at least 6 ft (2 m) from the ball until it is in play.

All free-kicks (except penalty kicks) given against the defending side for infringements committed in or near the goal area, shall be taken from a distance of not less from 6 ft (2 m) outside the goal area at the nearest point to where the offence occurred.

14. Penalty Kick: A penalty kick shall be taken from the penalty mark and except the defending goalkeeper, only the player taking the kick can enter the goal area and for that purpose only.

Whether or not a goal is scored from the kick, the player concerned must leave the goal area immediately and before taking any further part in play.

15. Goalkeeper Returning the Ball into Play: After holding the ball the goalkeeper must immediately return the ball into play with an underarm bowling action. It must not be thrown or kicked and it must be kept below head height.

Penalty for infringement: An indirect free-kick shall be taken by a player of the opposing team from a spot 6 ft (2 m) outside the goal area nearest to where the infringement occurred.

16. Play Within the Goal Area:

(a) Only the defending goalkeeper is allowed within the goal area, except when a penalty kick has been awarded and then only the player taking the kick can enter the goal area.

If a goalkeeper leaves the goal area he is then treated as any other player.

Penalty for infringement:

(i) By the attack – a direct free-kick at the point of entry into the goal area

(ii) By the defence – a penalty kick

Note: Referees should distinguish between accidental and intentional entry into or exit from the goal area. Only deliberate actions where the player either plays the ball or tries to play the ball should be penalised. Accidental entry or exit which has no effect on the play should be ignored.

17. Throw-Ins, Goal Kicks, Corner Kicks: There are no goal kicks, corners or throw-ins.

Appendix 2

Issued by the Football League:

Soccer Six

Except where otherwise stated, the Laws of Association Football shall apply.

1. The Playing Area:

(a) *Dimensions* – The maximum length of the playing area shall be 200 ft and the minimum length 175 ft. The maximum width shall be 90 ft and the minimum width 80 ft. The four corners shall be rounded.

(b) *Perimeter Boards* – The playing area shall be enclosed by fibreglass or wooden boards surrounded by plexiglass or similar material. The boards shall be 3 ft high and the plexiglass 4 ft high, except along each goal-line between the corner flags where the plexiglass shall be 6 ft high.

(c) *Goals* – Each goal shall be 12 ft wide and and 6 ft 6 ins high. The goals shall be built into the perimeter boards so that the goalposts are flush with the board's surface.

(d) *Playing Surface* – The playing surface shall be of an approved artificial material which shall be green in colour.

(e) *Pitch Markings* –

(i) Touch Lines — A broken line shall be drawn parallel to the perimeter boards 3 ft inside the playing area. This line shall terminate with a corner mark at a point level with the outer edge of the goalkeeper's area, i.e. 5 ft from an undrawn extension of the goal-line.

A corner flag, the top of which shall be raised to a height of 3 ft above the plexiglass shall be placed at the point along the perimeterboards where an undrawn extention of the

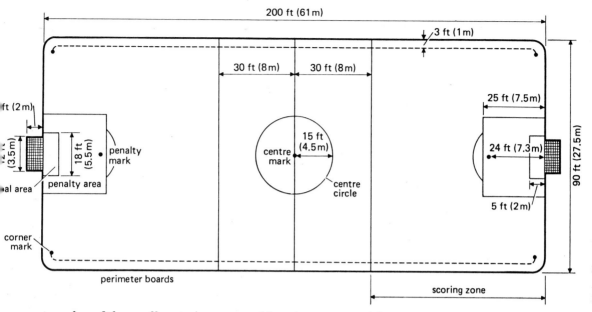

200 ft (61 m)

3 ft (1 m)

30 ft (8 m)   30 ft (8 m)

25 ft (7.5 m)

ft (2 m)

18 ft (5.5 m)

(3.5 m)

penalty mark

penalty area

al area

corner mark

perimeter boards

15 ft (4.5 m)

centre mark

centre circle

24 ft (7.3 m)

5 ft (2 m)

90 ft (27.5 m)

scoring zone

outer edge of the goalkeeper's area would make contact with the perimeter boards.

(ii) Centre circle — The centre circle shall have a radius of 15 ft.

(iii) Goalkeeper's Area — Each goalkeeper's area shall extend into the playing area a distance of 5 ft from the goal-lines and 3 ft from each goal post.

A penalty mark shall be placed at a point 24 ft from the centre of each goal-line. An arc shall be drawn outside each penalty area a distance of 10 ft from the penalty mark.

(iv) Scoring Zone — A red and white line shall be drawn in each half of the playing area a distance of 30 ft from, and parallel with, the halfway line. The area between this line and the goal-line shall be called the scoring zone.

2. The Ball: The specification of the ball shall be as approved by the The Football League.

3. Number of Players: Each team shall consist of a maximum ten players, not more than six of whom may be operative at any one time. The players who are inoperative may act as substitutes at any time during the game (without necessarily waiting for the ball to go out of play). There is no limit to the number of times any player may act as substitute. A match shall not be considered valid if there are fewer than four players.

4. Players' Equipment: The players' shirts shall be clearly numbered from one to ten. Goalkeepers may wear tracksuits which are clearly distinguishable from the colours worn by all other players. Light footwear suitable for the indoor surface shall be worn.

5. Referees: The referee shall have the same duties and powers as laid down in the Laws of Association Football except those expressly mentioned in Rule 6 below.

6. Other Match Officials: An additional official shall be positioned outside the playing area at the halfway line in order to ensure that the provisions of Laws 14 and 15 are observed. In the event of any infringement he will signal to the referee.

Additional officials will supervise the players' enclosures and sin bins. A record-keeper shall also be appointed to:

(a) act as time-keeper (including the supervision of time on instruction from the referee);

(b) record the goals, and

(c) signal half-time and full-time.

7. Duration of the Game: The duration of the game shall be two equal periods of ten minutes, subject to an allowance being made in either period for all time lost through stoppages. The half-time interval shall not exceed two minutes except by consent of the referee.

Drawn games: In the event of scores being level at full-time, the winning team shall be determined by a penalty competition conducted as follows:

(a) the referee shall choose the goal at which all of the kicks shall be taken,

(b) the referee shall toss a coin to decide which team takes the first kick,

(c) each team shall take alternate kicks against the opposing goalkeeper (maximun six),

(d) each kick shall be taken by a player who was on the field of play at the final whistle including the goalkeepers,

(e) a player who is in the sin bin at the end of a game shall be eligible to take a penalty kick, but a player who is sent off shall be disqualified from participating in the penalty competition,

(f) the team scoring the most penalties shall be declared the winners,

(g) in the event of the scores still being level after each player has taken one kick, an additional penalty shall be taken by each team until the scores differ, and

(h) the players taking additional penalties shall be in the same order as before.

8. The Start of Play: At the start of play the ball may be played in any direction.

Every player of the team opposing that of the kicker shall remain not less than 15 ft from the ball.

After any stoppage not specifically mentioned in these rules, the game shall be restarted by the referee dropping the ball (unless the ball was in the goalkeeper's possession, in which case the game shall be restarted by the goalkeeper throwing the ball into play). The referee shall not drop the ball within 6 ft of the penalty area or perimeter boards.

9. Ball In and Out of Play: The ball shall be regarded as out of play when the timekeeper has given the signal for full-time or half-time.

In the event of the ball being played over the perimeter boards alongside the touch-line, a player of the opposing team shall take a place kick from the touch-line at the point where the ball crossed the boards. A goal may not be scored directly from a touch-line place kick.

When a member of the attacking team plays the ball over the perimeter boards on the goal-line, the ball shall be thrown back into play by the defending goalkeeper. When a member of the defending team plays the ball over the perimeter boards on the goal-line, the attacking team shall take a corner kick.

10. Method of Scoring: A goal may only be scored from

within the respective scoring zones. In the event of the ball entering the goal from outside the scoring zone, without touching a player inside the zone, a goal shall not be awarded and the goalkeeper shall throw the ball back into play.

A goal shall not be allowed if the ball is last played by a player of the attacking team whilst being within the goalkeeper's area. (If the ball was last played by a defender whilst being within his own goalkeeper's area, a goal shall be allowed.)

11. Fouls and Misconduct: There shall be no restriction as to the height the ball may be played. In the event of the ball hitting the ceiling an indirect free-kick shall be awarded against the offending player.

Charging is forbidden and shall be penalised by the awarding of a direct free-kick.

A player shall be sent to the sin bin for two minutes if:

(a) he persistently infringes these rules, or

(b) he shows by word or action, dissent from any decision given by the referee, or

(c) he is guilty of ungentlemanly conduct.

Deliberate delays of the game will also be penalised by the offending player serving two minutes in the sin bin. These include:

(d) a player who deliberately puts the ball over the perimeter boards and out of play,

(e) a player who, having received the ball from his own goalkeeper, immediately returns it to the goalkeeper without the ball being touched by another player,

(f) a defending player who encroaches within 10 ft of the ball at free-kicks,

(g) a goalkeeper who fails to distribute the ball within five seconds.

For any of these last seven offences, in addition to the sin bin punishment, an indirect free-kick shall also be awarded to the opposing side from the place where the offence occurred, unless a more serious infringement of rules was committed.

A player shall be sent off the field of play if:

(a) in the opinion of the referee, he is guilty of violent conduct of serious foul play, or

(b) he uses foul or abusive language, or

(c) he persists in misconduct after having served two minutes in the sin bin.

If play is stopped by reason of a player being ordered from the field for an offence without a separate breach of these rules having been committed, the game shall be resumed by an indirect free-kick awarded to the opposite side from the place where the infringement occurred.

Substitutes shall not be allowed to replace a player in the sin bin or a player who has been sent off.

12. Free Kick: When a player is taking a direct or indirect free-kick, all of the opposing players shall be at least 10 ft from the ball, until it is in play. Indirect free-kicks given against the defending team for infringements committed inside their own penalty area shall be taken from outside the penalty area, at the nearest point to where the offence occurred.

13. Penalty Kick: At the taking of a penalty kick, all players except the penalty taker and the defending goal-keeper shall be at least 10 ft from the penalty mark.

14. Three Line Rule: In the event of the ball being played across the two red and white lines and the centre line without touching the playing surface or another player, an indirect free-kick shall be awarded against the offending player.

15. Player in Opposing Half: Within five seconds of the kick-off or re-start of a game, a minimum of one player from each team must remain in the opponent's half of the field. The punishment for an infringement shall be a penalty kick.

This rule shall not apply in the event of a team having less than six players on the field.

16. Play Within the Goalkeeper's Area: Only the goal-keepers are allowed within their respective areas. The punishment for an infringement is:

(a) by a defender – penalty kick

(b) by an attacker – goalkeeper's ball.

Note: Referees shall distinguish between accident and intentional entry into the goalkeeper's area. Only deliberate actions where the player interferes or attempts to interfere with the game shall be penalised.

Appendix 3

Summary on the **Condensed Rules of Indoor Soccer** as administered by the North American Soccer League:

1. The Playing Field: Length, width and goals as for Soccer six. Goal area 16 ft wide × 5 ft from endline. Penalty area 30 ft by 25 ft. Penalty mark and arc as for Soccer Six.

2. The Ball: As used in the outdoor game.

3. Number of Players: A team can list a maximum of fourteen players, with a maximum of six and minimum of four on the field at any one time. Substitutions are unlimited but play will be held up for completion of a substitution only after a goal, after a time penalty award, injury stoppages, or when the ball has crossed the goal or touchline over the perimeter wall.

4. Equipment: Players must wear flat sole shoes or moulded sole shoes with no less than ten mini studs.

5. The Referee: One referee shall officiate each game.

6. Assistant Referee: To assist the referee in control of the game and keep a record of the game and time penalties.

7. Duration of the Game: Four equal periods of fifteen minutes. If teams are level at the end of normal time, the game will be extended by fifteen minute periods of 'sudden death' overtime until one team scores. The clock will be stopped with every referee's whistle and shall not be restarted until the ball has travelled half the distance of its circumference.

8. Start of Play: the visiting team kick off for the first and third quarters, the home team in the second and fourth. Home team has choice of ends at the start. The teams change around at each quarter.

Ball In and Out of Play: When it has wholly crossed goal-line or perimeter wall, or when the game has been stopped by the referee. Otherwise the ball is in play, including rebounds off referee, perimenter wall, goal post, etc.

10. Method of Scoring: When the whole of the ball passes completely over the goal line, between posts and under the bar.

11. Three-Line Pass Violation: This occurs when the ball passes three lines marked across the pitch (one in each half at 30 ft from the centre line) in the air without touching the perimeter wall, the floor or a player. An indirect free-kick is awarded against the player involved. Any team playing with two players fewer than the opposing team shall not be penalised for this offence.

12. Fouls and Misconduct: Major infractions are penalised by a direct free-kick and, if the infraction is serious enough, by a two-minute time penalty (in the sin bin).

A player shall be sent off if, in the opinion of the referee, he is guilty of serious foul play or violent conduct, uses foul or abusive languague, or persists in misconduct having previously been cautioned.

A goalkeeper, having had control of the ball in his hands and having released it, shall not handle the ball again until it has been touched or played by an opponent, unless a stoppage or play occurs. Infringement incurs an indirect free-kick. Any two-minute time penalties assessed against a goalkeeper are served by another member of his team.

A team reduced to fewer players than the opposing side, because of time penalties, can, once a goal is conceded, immediately bring back into play the player having served the longest of his unexpired time penalty.

13. Free Kicks: The kicker shall have five seconds within which to play the ball after being signalled to do so by the referee. Failure to comply will result in a two-minute time penalty in the sin bin. But his team maintains the right to continue with the taking of the free kick.

14. Penalty Kicks: All players, except kicker and goal-keeper, must be outside the penalty box. The kicker may not play the ball a second time, if it rebounds from post, bar or perimeter wall, until it has been touched by another player.

15. Kick In: When the ball passes over the perimeter wall it shall be kicked in from the point where it crossed the dotted touchline which is marked 3 ft from the perimeter wall. A goal cannot be scored direct.

16. Goal Kick: An indirect kick awarded when the ball has passed over the perimeter goal line after being last touched by an attacking player.

17. Corner Kick: A direct free kick taken from the corner mark closest to where the ball went out of play.

Appendix 4

Championship Winners

Standard London Five-a-Side Championship

1954	Charlton	1972	QPR
1955	Fulham	1973	Chelsea
1956	Spurs	1974	QPR
1957	Fulham	1975	Charlton
1958	Orient	1976	Orient
1959	Crystal Palace	1977	Arsenal
1960	Spurs	1978	Millwall
	Tournament suspended	1979	Millwall
1967	West Ham	1980	QPR
1968	Charlton	1981	Arsenal
1969	Crystal Palace	1982	Fulham
1970	West Ham	1983	Millwall
1971	QPR	1984	West Ham

Daily Express Five-a-Side National Football Championship

1968	Charlton Athletic	1976	Wolves
1969	Manchester City	1977	Ipswich
1970	Manchester United	1978	Crystal Palace
1971	Southampton	1979	Sunderland
1972	Tottenham Hotspur	1980	Aston Villa
1973	Derby County	1981	Celtic
1974	Orient	1982	Arsenal
1975	Wolves	1983	Southampton

Sponsored Soccer Six Tournament
Arranged in association with the Football League

1982	Birmingham City	(Midlands teams only, pilot tournament)
1983	Birmingham City	(Atari Sponsored)
1984	Arsenal	(Courage/Birmingham City Council Sponsored)